# Emily Murphy

**Donna James**

Fitzhenry & Whiteside Limited

# Contents

## THE CANADIANS
*A Continuing Series*

## Emily Murphy

*Author:* Donna James
*Design:* Kerry Designs
*Cover Illustration:* John Mardon

Fitzhenry & Whiteside acknowledge with thanks the support of the Government of Canada
through its Book Publishing Industry Development Program.
**Canadian Cataloguing in Publication Data**
James, Donna
Emily Murphy
(The Canadians) Rev. ed.
Includes bibliographical references and index.
ISBN 1-55041-491-7
1. Murphy, Emily F. (Emily Ferguson), 1868-1933. 2. Women judges-Canada-Biography. 3. Feminists-Canada-Biography. 4. Authors,
Canadian (English)-Biography.* I. Title. II. Series.

FC541.M7J36 2000                    971.061'092                    C00-930543-2
F1034.M87J36 2000

© 2001 Fitzhenry & Whiteside Limited
195 Allstate Parkway, Markham, Ontario L3R 4T8

# Chapter 1
# Childhood

Emily Ferguson was born in 1868 in the village of Cookstown in southern Ontario. She grew into a boisterous child, forever getting into mischief with her older brothers, Thomas and Gowan. Dressed in smocks and sturdy lace-up boots, her thick pigtails flying in the wind, she spent her days exploring the woods and fields beyond the family garden.

She often went fishing with her brothers in a nearby beaver dam. They caught suckers and sunfish that they would string on a branch of willow to carry home like trophies. In the fall, when maple leaves turned crimson, they would sneak home with other prizes to hide in the woodpile – apples stolen from a neighbour's orchard. There were plenty of apples on their own trees, but where was the adventure in that? No, it was much more exciting to plan a raid and run the risk of being caught – which they were on more than one occasion.

Their father would sternly march the boys into the house and down the hall to the storage room at the far end. Closing the door, he left Emily outside cringing with sympathy for her brothers every time she heard the crack of the whip.

It was custom in the 1870s to use the whip and it did not mean that Isaac Ferguson was a cruel father. He loved his children and wanted them to become strong and independent. He encouraged his daughter to do the things her brothers did. Emily played cricket, rode astride and took care of her own pony, and was able to hitch and drive a team of horses. She was also expected to help with the chores – piling wood for winter and weeding the vegetable garden. Her mother was dismayed by this tomboy daughter. She had been taught to be a "lady," and a lady would never stoop to soil her hands in a garden. This conflict between mother and daughter persisted throughout their lives.

*Isaac Ferguson, Emily's father*

*Dr. Gowan Ferguson*

*Thomas Ferguson, K.C.*

Emily's mother, also named Emily, grew up at a time when young women were forbidden to read about politics or business because it was believed that worldly knowledge would corrupt the purity of their minds. "Don't bother your pretty little head about that," she would be told – and she did what she was told. Not expected to have a career, she had been trained instead to fit the role of wife and mother, and to become a lovely adornment for her husband. As a girl, she spent hours making herself attractive – curling her hair and arranging it in hundreds of tiny braids. She wore hooped underskirts designed to reveal a glimpse of ruffles and lace when she danced the Polish mazurka. Her wealth protected her from the evils of the world and, like other women of her background, she was ignorant of the conditions under which most women lived.

The younger Emily grew up to have a very different life. She saw and heard things of which her mother never dreamed. Yet she always maintained an image of her, unchanging like a photograph from the past, that expressed the beautiful things her mother represented. She wrote, "I can see my mother, with her dark hair brushed smoothly back and circling her head in a coronet of braids. It was in the spring, for I remember she stood under the lilac bushes and they were in bloom." This image of serenity haunted Emily whenever she saw the poverty and degradation of others.

However, this aspect of the world was far from Emily's mind when, as a young girl, she was allowed to sit in the parlour and watch the visiting ladies taking tea. The women drank from dainty flowered cups and made polite conversation. Sometimes, if the weather was cold, the wine decanter would be produced for the guests to take a few discreet sips of cherry brandy. They preferred to call it fruit punch.

Isaac Ferguson was a wealthy landowner and businessman. He and his wife enjoyed entertaining friends in their large, rambling home. An occasional guest was Sir John A. Macdonald, Canada's first prime minister. He was a friend of Emily's grandfather, Ogle R. Gowan. Mr. Gowan owned several newspapers and had been a politician in the Conservative party for 27 years.

The Ferguson home was situated on the edge of Cookstown in a grove of maple trees. The dirt road to the village was scarred with deep ruts and bumps. In

**Childhood**

spring it was bogged down in mud; in winter it was treacherous with ice and snow-drifts. There were no motorcars in the 1870s and people travelled in horse-drawn carriages. The family carriage was known as *The Chariot* because the children drove it as if they were in a Roman amphithe-atre. "There go them young Fergu-son devils," the neighbours would say.

Punished for their careless dri-ving, the children would find new ways of getting into trouble. When they grew older, Thomas and Gowan would hide in the hayloft and secretly smoke elm root. Unwanted, Emily retreated to the woodshed to con-fide in her favourite

*Sir John A. Macdonald*

china doll. By this time she had a younger brother, William, and a baby sister, Annie.

At age seven, Emily was sent to the local school where she met the village children. The school was made entirely of wood, was painted red, and had only one room in which children of all ages sat and learned together. Desks and benches were carved by hand, and ink bottles were made of stone. In winter the older pupils were responsi-ble for filling the pot-bellied stove with wood.

*Ogle R. Gowan, Emily's grandfather*

Isaac Ferguson planned to send his children to private schools in Toronto. To prepare them for this, he arranged extra lessons that were not taught in the one-room schoolhouse. The local rector agreed to instruct the children in Latin. Incredible as it may seem, their father hired a tutor to come all the way from Barrie, a 26 km journey made every Saturday morning, just to teach the children penmanship. The idea was not to have them write with ornamental flourishes, but to teach them how to hold the pen properly so they could write for hours without getting cramped fingers. He also insisted on music lessons, and Emily spent many hours practising on the piano in the parlour.

The Fergusons were well known to the people of Cookstown because Emily's grandfather was somewhat of a local hero. Ogle R. Gowan, like most of the villagers, was of Irish Protestant background. At that time in English-speaking Canada there was a great deal of religious strife. Protestants and Catholics had a long history of political antagonism. Following the Battle of the Boyne in Ireland in 1690 (a bloody fight between Catholic Ireland and Protestant England) some Protestants got together to form a society called the Orange Order. Every 12th of July they celebrated the defeat of Ireland by holding an Orange Day Parade. When Emily's grandfather came to Canada he wanted to continue this tradition, so he founded a local branch of the Orange Order in 1830. Thus, every year on the eve of the parade, the

*Queen St., Cookstown, about 1912*

villagers put on a procession to honour his memory.

With a vocal family tradition like this, it is not surprising that Emily became involved in public issues. One of her uncles, Sir James Gowan, was a Supreme Court Judge and later a senator; another, Mr. Justice Thomas Ferguson, was Judge of the Ontario Supreme Court. During their visits, the conversation around the dinner table would inevitably turn to a discussion of law and current political events. The Ferguson children absorbed this information along with their dinner. The boys were expected to eventually have careers in politics or law, which they did. Thomas became a brilliant lawyer and William a member of the Supreme Court. But nobody thought at the time that young Emily would be the first woman in Canada ever to be appointed judge.

# Chapter 2
# Leaving Home

Emily was restless. She could not sleep. Outside her window some birds were chattering, but the rest of the house was still silent. She lay in bed looking around the room that was so familiar. Soon she would be sharing a dormitory with girls she did not know; she would have to get up when a bell rang, whether she liked it or not.

Hanging on a hook by the door was her new school uniform. Emily jumped out of bed, washed quickly in a bowl of cold water, then brushed and braided her long dark hair. She put on the green woollen dress, buttoned up her high polished boots, and was ready to go. At the age of 14, small and slim, her childhood was over. She was leaving home to attend boarding school in Toronto.

Set amid lawns and playing field, Bishop Strachan School was an exclusive grammar school for the daughters of wealthy families. It was the female equivalent to Upper Canada College, where Emily's brothers went. Based on the British public school system, and supported by the Anglican Church, both schools were criticized by nineteenth-century reformers for being elitist.

Bishop Strachan was certainly very different from the country school in Cookstown. Discipline was strictly enforced and pupils had to show respect for their teacher by standing whenever she entered the room, and by opening the door for her when she left. Subjects were taught by memorization and repetition. Emily developed a remarkable memory which later inspired Nellie McClung, the ardent feminist, to describe her mind as encyclopedic.

Emily received a classical education with a heavy emphasis on religious knowledge. "It was truly a wistful, incongruous picture, this of the little country girl tingling with life in every vein, parroting stately words and squirming out the hour of catechism and instruction."

The experience of being taught religion in a mechanical way had a deep effect on Emily. She would always make a distinction between the true spirit of religion and the hypocrisy and rules that surrounded it.

Every Sunday, the whole school, pupils and teachers, would set off in a dignified procession toward the Anglican Cathedral of St. James on the lakeshore. These walks wound through quiet, shady streets, where families sat in rocking chairs on front porches. Horse-drawn carriages clipped by, carrying people dressed in their Sunday best to church.

Toronto was already a big and growing city. It had two large department stores on Yonge Street – Eaton's and Simpsons – and industry was expanding. Along the lakeshore, new factories were beginning to spring up beside the tangled network of railway tracks and sidings. These factories, each employing about a hundred people, were investigated by the federal government in 1882. It was discovered that in some of them, eight-year-old children worked as much as ten hours a day under shocking conditions. The children operated dangerous and temperamental steam engines in dark, windowless rooms where the air was thick with dust and fumes. Machines were run without safety devices and sometimes caused gruesome accidents when little hands and arms were caught and mangled in them.

Wages were pitifully low. Children who worked in these factories lived in squalid slums. Many people relied on alcohol as a temporary escape from the horrors of daily life – but alcohol abuse only increased the agony. The violence that drunkenness caused within families created intolerable situations that were publicly denounced by religious groups and reformers. Several temperance organizations were formed as a result. The most powerful and articulate was the Women's Christian Temperance Union.

Safe at Bishop Strachan, it was hard to imagine such things existed. Emily studied hard and her report cards usually read "works admirably." Her favourite subjects were literature, botany and sports. Saturdays provided a relief from school work. Thomas and Gowan came from nearby Upper Canada College to take Emily out for the afternoon.

*Extremes in living conditions in Montreal, about 1912*

*A billboard advertisement*                    *St. Lawrence Hall, Toronto, 1885*

Through a school friend Emily had been introduced to a young man who was a student at Wycliffe College in Toronto. Arthur Murphy planned to become a minister in the Anglican Church. He was 26 at the time and Emily only 15. She was intrigued by this older man, and flattered that he was interested in her. Years later she wrote, "I fell in love many times in my teens, but there was never anyone, really, but Arthur."

They arranged to meet secretly with the help of her brothers. Thomas and Gowan still came to call for her at school, but Arthur was waiting around the corner, and he and Emily would go off together for the afternoon. They would ferry across to the Toronto Islands which were very popular recreation spots even then. Families had built summer homes along the shore, and wooden hotels on Hanlan's Point provided refreshments and music. There were several boat clubs, and a small amusement park. Nobody swam in public because the Victorian attitudes of the 1880s did not favour bathing costumes. But there was another reason, less genteel, that prohibited swimming. The lake was known to be polluted because raw sewage was dumped into it.

At times, Emily would remember the clear river in Cookstown where she used to fish with her brothers. She began to look forward to holidays at home, and wrote to her parents describing the handsome young man she had met, mentioning his startling blue eyes, his fair

*A regatta off Toronto Island, 1888*

**Leaving home** 11

*Arthur Murphy*

hair. Recognizing an infatuation, the Fergusons decided to invite Arthur to Cookstown so they could look him over. He met with their approval.

On August 23, 1887, Arthur Murphy and Emily Ferguson married in Cookstown's Anglican Church.

An odd thing happened the night before the wedding. Emily was alone in the house, which was dark except for an oil lamp in the hall that gave off feeble light. She descended the stairs dressed in her white satin wedding gown and lace veil. Standing before the marble-based mirror in the hall, she studied her reflection. It was too dark to see clearly so she moved the lamp closer to the mirror. There was a sudden crack and explosion that ripped through the silence. Emily screamed. The heat from the lamp had shattered the old mirror. "My mother had the mirror covered with curtains that the guests might not see, but the guests saw, and more than one woman looked at me with curious, half-frightened eyes." For the superstitious, the cracked mirror was an omen.

That was Emily's last night at home. The house was never the same again. A few years after the wedding, Isaac Ferguson became ill and died of cancer. His wife decided to sell the family home and move to Toronto where the children attended school – Gowan in medicine, Thomas and William in law at Osgoode Hall, Annie at Bishop Strachan, and Harcourt at Upper Canada College. Several months later, the house caught fire and burned to the ground. Not a trace of it was left standing.

# Chapter 3
# A Parson's Wife

Life in the small towns of southern Ontario was conservative and secure for most people in the 1880s. Religion was an important part of social life and nearly everyone went to church at least once a week. The local parson and his wife were expected to set a good example for their flock. The behaviour of the parson's wife was watched closely. If she happened to depart from a rigid code of respectability, she might be shunned by the older women in the community.

It was not easy for Emily to turn into a model parson's wife overnight. At 19, she was much younger than any of the women she was supposed to guide. Spontaneous and direct with people, she was quick to recognize and ridicule pretensions of any kind. Her unconventional behaviour got her into trouble a few times, as happened when she discovered that one of her servants went to church too often – six times a week. The woman became depressed about her sins and frequently burst into tears while working about the house. Emily's solution: "I cut off three meetings and substituted a course of modern fiction – largely humorous. The results are clearly salutary, but in certain church circles it was whispered that I am a monster of wickedness and tyranny."

Emily showed common sense, humour, and a genuine concern for others in all her dealings with people. She had no time for a religion that talked only of the world to come, but believed instead that it was the duty of religion to teach us how to live now. Her overflowing joy in living caused her to remark, "I am possessed with a pagan love of life."

Emily made good use of her experience as a parson's wife. She developed a flair for leadership in organizing groups of women to work together on projects. She arranged and co-ordinated fundraising events, spoke at meetings, taught Bible classes, and was president of the Missionary Society. All these activities were good training for the social work she would eventually do in Western Canada.

For ten years the Murphys moved from one small town in Ontario to another. Respected for his preaching and community work, Arthur was also admired for his business talents. He managed the financial aspects of his work so well that once he had set up a church and it was operating smoothly, he was asked to leave and revive a failing church somewhere else.

One of the towns in which they lived was Chatham. It had been a haven for fugitive American slaves who crossed the Canadian border. In fact, one third of Chatham's population was African American. These American-born fugitives were employed in the homes of white Canadians as gardeners, maids and cooks. A cook earned five dollars a week.

Emily shopped in the local outdoor market where there was an astounding variety of food. Women from the southern United States sold hominy and cured tobacco tied in twists and bundles. German women sold sauerkraut, russet apples, and a thick brown syrup made from sweet corn called sorghum. French women sold home-made cheese, silver honey in the wax, garden herbs and yellow squash. There were also turkeys, rabbits, geese, eggs, cream and celery.

These were tranquil years of domestic life in which Emily was supremely happy to be the mother of three daughters, Kathleen, Evelyn, and Doris. With a maid, and a nursemaid for the children, Emily had time for reading, oil painting, working in the parish, and researching stories for Arthur's sermons. She was not content to be a mother only. "We are coming to see that a mother who lets herself subside into a kind of burnt-sacrifice upon what is called the 'family altar' is not really a good mother, nor a good citizen." Of course the hired help made motherhood easier.

This settled time in their lives came to an abrupt end. Arthur, the restless visionary, was looking for new adventure. He found it. The local bishop asked him if he would be willing to give up his home to become a missionary. Arthur could not resist a new challenge.

Emily supported him in his decision although she was sad to leave her home and friends. Her mother was very upset and accused Arthur of being a nomad, irresponsibly uprooting his wife and children. But her words were useless – the furniture was sold, the clothes packed, and the whole family took off for parts unknown.

The horse-drawn carriage clipped along country roads carrying the Reverend Arthur Murphy and his family on to the next town. For Emily, the countryside, fields, grey barns, trees, log cabins and yellow brick houses blurred into one long repetition. The villages they passed all looked the same to her now. New faces on the streets merged into a continuous parade of strangers.

Emily missed the old life. She had enjoyed having a home of her own and the friendship of neighbours. It was different now: always travelling, moving from one town to another every two weeks, staying in a series of small hotels. She was a stranger wherever she went.

She began watching people and places very closely. To make sense out of these new impressions she started to keep a diary. Emily had a knack for seeing the humorous side of situations and the foibles of human nature. Soon she was writing every day – on any scrap of paper available when something caught her imagination.

A year passed. The Mission Society heard about Arthur's excellent work, and impressed by his dedication, they offered him a chance to preach in England. England!

*Arthur and Emily with Evelyn, Doris and Kathleen*

**A Parson's Wife**

# Chapter 4
# Janey Canuck Goes Travelling

In the summer of 1898, the Murphys set sail for England. For two years they travelled about the country, saw many cities, made many friends. But by the time they left, many of their illusions about the mother country had been shattered.

While Arthur was preaching and the children were in school, Emily had time to explore on her own. She visited places she had read about in history books – the dungeons in the Tower of London, the British Museum, Speakers' Corner at Hyde Park. A favourite attraction in London was a ride down the river Thames in a pleasure steamer. Among the crowd of tourists there was one girl who stood apart. People glanced at her curiously then turned away in embarrassment. Her face was horribly disfigured.

Emily approached the girl and started a conversation. Her friendly manner gained the girl's trust. After a few minutes, Emily asked what had happened to her face. The girl explained that she had been working in a match factory. The air was constantly filled with phosphorus fumes that eventually caused a disease known as matchmaker's leprosy. "The teeth ache and then drop out. Later the loathsome leprosy eats its way into the roof of the mouth, and inside the nose, and then the jaw drops off. They sometimes lose their sight before death. The girl's wages were $1.92 a week. Who is responsible?"

Emily was changing and learning. In Ontario, she had never seen the brutal poverty that existed in the industrial cities of England. It was not in her nature to witness an injustice and then walk away. She had to do something about it. The weapon she chose was writing – writing that would shock people out of their complacency. In England she wrote her first book and called it *Impressions of Janey Canuck Abroad.*

Unable to accept surface appearances, she strayed away from the historic sites and wandered through the back alleys and poor districts where most tourists never went. She wrote bitterly about "the foul atmosphere of fetid slums and rotting tenements." She described crumbling buildings smelling of dirt and disease, places where garbage littered dark hallways and damp, dingy stairs. She saw men in rags tapping up and down the narrow streets, begging for money. Some were

soldiers who had been horribly wounded in the Boer War of 1899–1902. What was being done for them? Was this their reward for fighting overseas in South Africa?

*Filling cans with Damson Plum Jam, E.D. Smith's, Winona, Ontario, 1911*

Emily's social conscience had been aroused. Industrialization was more advanced in Victorian England than it was in Canada. Most Canadians still lived in the country and many were independent farmers. But in Britain, people were crowded into dirty cities, forced to work in sweatshops where the wages were barely enough to keep them alive. Emily was outraged by the extremes in wealth, and believed that Britain's class system made it inevitable that the poor would always remain so.

Away from home for the first time, she began to see Canada in a different light. Of course there were social distinctions in Canada too, but they were less binding and rigid. Immigrants could arrive with almost nothing and build a life in the new cities, or acquire a homestead, construct a house from wood or stone, breed animals and plant crops. With very hard work and some help from the weather, newcomers had a chance of one day owning a prospering farm. The Canadian government was advertising all over Europe for immigrants to come and work the land. People were desperately needed to plough the soil, build roads, develop new industries, construct cities. It did not make sense that Britain, a tiny island, had people starving to death and homeless, while Canada, the second largest country in the world, had room for thousands.

Standing on the dock in Liverpool waiting to board the ship that would take them home, Emily looked around for the last time at the scene she was leaving. Spirals of black smoke curled upwards from factory chimneys, then disappeared into a heavy mass of dark cloud that slowly advanced over the city. Her eyes swept down to the harbour where gulls dove for scraps of bread and rubbish that drifted on the dull water. The sun emerged briefly. The noise and chatter of people on the crowded wharves began to sound festive. She watched the hurrying mass of immigrants surging up the gangplank and onto the boat, old people and young, families with babies and bundles on their backs. They were going to the New World, in one gesture casting off their old lives of poverty and despair, gambling everything on the hope that in Canada, they could build a better life for their children. Emily wished them well. It was a long journey by sea and then by train to the heartland of Canada. Eastern Canada had long been settled, and these people were going to the new frontier, to the great grasslands of the prairies. Emily Murphy, writer, would follow them within three years.

Whistle shrieking, the train

*Poster dated 1869 displayed in Europe and Eastern Canada*

steamed into Toronto, then clanged to a noisy halt at the station. Some passengers descended, the Murphys among them, and milled around the platform, amid the confusion of frantic relatives and porters running to and fro with luggage. Emily was tired. Looking back at the departing train, at the grey-faced immigrants staring through the dusty windows on their long journey west, she felt no desire to go with them. After years of travelling, she was relieved to be home again, to have solid ground under her feet.

*Advertising campaign to lure immigrants to Canada's shores.*

Emerging from the dark station into glaring sunlight, it was a shock to see how the city had changed since her schooldays at Bishop Strachan. Main roads were now paved in gleaming concrete. Electric streetcars clattered past horse-drawn carriages. Telephone poles and wires made a tangled network overhead. Emily even glimpsed some new apartment buildings rising awkwardly above groups of smaller houses. Yet, despite the changes, familiar landmarks remained, and Toronto was still home.

The Murphy's found a pleasant house near High Park. Arthur continued his work with the Mission Society. Kathleen and Evelyn went to school at Havergal College and, with only young Doris at home, Emily was free to pursue her own career.

The book she wrote in Britain, *Impressions of Janey Canuck Abroad*, was published in 1901. It reached a small audience but won much praise for its honest description of social problems. Emily wrote in a flowing style that was easy to read and very entertaining. In Toronto she started writing for small magazines under a variety of pen names – Lady Jane, The Duchess, Earlie York. She did book reviews and wrote about housekeeping and fashions. Her favourite time for writing was at midnight when the city was silent and she was alone with her thoughts.

One night Arthur came home pale and feverish. "Just a cold," he reassured Emily. "I'll be fine by morning." But the next day he was flushed and delirious. Emily sent for the family doctor. Waiting uneasily in the living room downstairs, she heard the bedroom door open and close, heard measured steps descending the stairs, then crossing the hall. She rose from her chair and turned to the doctor as he entered the room. From his expression, she knew at once the news was bad. "He has typhoid," the doctor said.

Arthur hovered between life and death for months. The Mission Society, on the verge of bankruptcy, wrote to say they could no longer afford to pay his salary. With no money coming in, the bills piled up with terrifying speed. In order to pay them, Emily worked through the nights turning out articles and book reviews for magazines. Nursing Arthur by day and writing all night, her strength began to fade and she too came down with *the fever*. Much later, recovering in hospital, she wrote *The Diary of a Typhoid Patient*. It helped pay her medical expenses.

Young Doris had missed her very much. In the afternoons, mother and daughter went to High Park where Emily, wrapped in warm blankets, sat on a bench recuperating in the sun. She watched Doris running through the grass, throwing scraps of bread to feed the pigeons and

*Toronto 1907, looking north on Avenue Road at Davenport*

Janey Canuck Goes Travelling

squirrels that formed a circle around them. It was Indian summer, that strange time of year when two seasons are present at once. A brilliant autumn sun shone through the pale transparent leaves, casting an eerie glow upon the grass, outlining the shapes of trees and faces in a shimmering light. The smell of damp moss rose up from the earth.

The weather grew colder and the long afternoons in the park came to an end. One bleak morning in November, Doris woke up with a high fever. She thrashed about in bed, rising and sinking in waves of delirium. "Try not to worry," advised the doctor. "She has diphtheria. With proper care she'll get over it."

*Immigrants waiting to go ashore at Quebec City, 1911*

*101 Street, looking north to immigration hall, Edmonton, Alberta, c.1912*

Emily nursed her endlessly, but despite all her efforts, the dreaded complications of diphtheria set in. On a dark day in December, Doris died in her sleep.

That winter dragged on like a nightmare. Weakened by their own recent illnesses, and overwhelmed by grief, the Murphys sank further and further into despair. The family doctor was an old friend and decided to intervene. Aware that Arthur owned a timber limit in northern Manitoba, he visited the Murphys one evening with a plan in mind. As they sat around the fire with the sound of wind wailing about the house, the doctor urged Arthur to give up church work, which was straining his health. "You should be outdoors in the fresh air. Why not pack up everything and go West? Develop your timber limit and make a new life for yourselves."

Emily's mother was horrified at the suggestion. "Why can't you stay in one place?" she protested. But the idea of a totally new setting, a challenge, and a pioneer way of life was something that gradually took hold of their imaginations. It was a dim light beckoning them through the dark winter months. When spring came, they packed up their possessions and said goodbye to family and friends.

"All aboard." Doors slammed, a whistle blew, and the train, westward bound, puffed out of the station. This time the Murphys were on it.

# Chapter 5
# Janey Canuck in the West

Thousands of immigrants poured into the Prairie provinces at the turn of the century. What did they see as they headed farther and farther into the unknown wilderness? One of them, Janey Canuck, described the journey.

*For miles and miles we pass over the great reach of the plains – the land where nothing meets but the four winds. It is a featureless, empty world that runs away into the sky in whatever direction you look....Nothing passes but the clouds; and yet they tell me this prairie wind's a glamour – a strange witchery about the heart that, travel where he may, no Westerner ever forgets or wishes to forget. Its weird sounds, and still more weird silences, become a part of his soul.*

*Emigrants leaving Minnesota for Western Canada*

The West became part of Emily's soul. She grew to love the land and its people. She admired the women and men for their courage and strength, for she believed that the gruelling conditions in a frontier society brought out the best in people.

Population 300, Swan River, Manitoba, was an isolated village typical of western

Swan River Town 1909

*Swan River, Manitoba*

settlements that were springing up overnight beside newly opened mines and railways. The settlers were too busy ploughing land, felling trees, mining metals, to do more than build for basic survival. The houses were ugly and square, like cardboard boxes. Hotels and stores were finished inside and out with painted tin. Swan River had several churches, a schoolhouse, real estate office, bank, barbershop and poolroom. But there was no hospital – at least not until Emily arrived on the scene.

She sent off a storm of letters to government officials, pointing out that a hospital was essential for the town and outlying home-steads. Her persistence finally paid off. Money was raised and the Victorian Order of Nurses' Hospital was built. In recognition of Emily Murphy's determined efforts, the town elected her president of the hospital board.

Emily explored the surrounding countryside on horseback. One time she visited a Native settlement and learned how to shoot with a bow and arrow. She chatted with farmers in the fields, visited hospitals, schools and jails. Her journeys took her farther afield by boat and train to gather material for stories that would explain the West to the rest of Canada.

She wrote three books about the frontier: *Janey Canuck in the West*,

*Open Trails*, and *Seeds of Pine*. These books contain stories told to her by Native people recounting ancient legends of the North; old-timers reminiscing about expeditions into the Yukon; missionaries recalling long years spent with the Inuit on remote shores of the Arctic. All tell of the struggle for survival in a harsh but beautiful land.

Emily's books resemble the literature of other pioneers, mostly women, who wrote in diaries or in letters about their lives in the Canadian wilderness, but each writer interpreted her experience differently. Susanna Moodie, for example, author of *Roughing It in the Bush*, immigrated to Upper Canada (Ontario) in 1832. Coming from the rigid class system of Britain, she found it very difficult to adapt to frontier society, where class origin meant little. Bound in tradition, she often wrote critically about the "lower-classes" and "foreigners." In contrast, Janey Canuck was as much at ease with a milkman as she was with a bishop. Believing immigrants were helping build Canada's future, she preferred to call them "coming Canadians."

*Susanna Moodie*

There were many heroes, men and women, who had done remarkable things in the frontier. Emily wrote a school history book about one of them, William Bompas. Bishop Bompas was an Anglican clergyman who had left England in 1868 to work as a missionary with the Inuit in the Arctic Circle. His 12-month journey by horse, boat, canoe, and then dog train was an incredible feat of endurance. In midwinter, with two French-speaking Cree guides, the trio cut their way through river-ice with axes. After 60 days on the river, they picked up a dog train and travelled for 30 more days to Fort Simpson on the Mackenzie River. Isolated from the industrialized world, Bishop Bompas felt he had gone far back into time. In their food, dress and customs, the Inuit lived the same way they had for centuries, for there was no need or desire for revolutionary change.

Bishop Bompas spent 40 years in the sole company of Aboriginal

*Bishop Bompas*

peoples. He translated and printed prayer books from English into seven Native languages. In spare moments he studied Greek and Hebrew. "But he was no mere bag of books," remarked Emily. He was also a man of action and great physical courage. In one summer he vaccinated 500 Native people against smallpox. As many as 2,000 had died of that disease the previous year.

While Emily travelled about the country writing stories and book reviews, Arthur worked on his timber limit which was near the Saskatchewan border. Anxious to see the camp for herself, Emily persuaded him to take her along on his next trip.

The morning for their departure dawned clear and cold with the temperature at –45°C. For two days they rode in an open sleigh, exposed to the harsh northern winter. Hour after hour they travelled on through vast blankets of snow. A lone moose crossed their path, perhaps drawn by the sound of sleigh bells. A snowy owl, perched on a dead stump, stared at them gravely. All was white except for a yellow band of the setting sun and grey tree shadows. Clusters of Lapland snowbirds rose up from the frosted trees to circle in the evening sky.

It was nightfall when they reached the Doukhobor village of Vosnesenia. The Murphys were hungry. Arthur fetched the food box from the sleigh and Emily fried some potatoes and bacon. The smell of sizzling meat offended the Doukhobors who were vegetarians. Some of the children walked around the kitchen holding their noses.

The Doukhobors lived simply and were self-sufficient. The women spun wool for weaving, dyed threads and made all clothes by hand. The whole village was like one big family – people visited each other in the evenings to sew, sing, or talk. All crops and money were shared equally. Like the Quakers, the Doukhobors believed in the principles of peace and love.

Women's work was respected as much as men's, for without it no family could survive. Emily noted, "The Doukhobor woman does not believe that her home is a jail, and that her babies are the turnkeys."

Convinced that motherhood was one of the most important roles in life, Emily firmly stressed that motherly love should not be confined within the family but should extend to everyone. Women could not even vote at this time, nor could they be politicians, lawyers, doctors, or members of any profession (save teaching). Emily believed that women should insist on taking an equal place with men so they could use their power to change society and improve the lives of all people.

She had studied ancient religions and knew that statues of female goddesses had been worshipped all over the world, long before

Judaism and Christianity. Referring to Roman Catholic statues of the Virgin Mary, Emily wrote: "In the ages that are to come it is possible that bloodless, long-fingered, weak-eyed scientists may, with wonder, dig Madonnas out of the earth just as today in Babylon, they dig up Istar, the goddess of childbirth. That for which the statue stands is eternal, and will always be worshipped, perhaps under another name."

After a few days in Vosnesenia, the Murphys travelled on. They passed through a spruce forest where streamers of moss, like the beards of old men, hung down from gnarled trees. Then came poplars covered in blotches of pale lichen.

Trees fell away and they entered a wasteland of burnt stumps and muskeg. The land grew more and more desolate. Timber wolves howled in the distance – a sinister sound echoing across empty space. With no shelter from the wind, Emily felt the Arctic cold seep into her body. Barely conscious by the time they reached camp, she had to be carried inside by two lumberjacks.

Gradually she revived in the warmth of the kitchen, and became aware of her new surroundings. The cook was telling a story about a missionary who had gone to stay with some Inuit. Unable to eat blubber, the missionary lived entirely on canned food. After a few months, *Doukhobor Village*

*Immigrant women performed invaluable labour in the fields and on the land as well as taking care of the house and children. Their life expectancy was shortened by overwork, inadequate medical care and complications arising in childbirth.*

he got a gramophone and played a record for the Inuit. No one spoke for half an hour. The one old man nudged another old man and nodded his head toward the gramophone as if he had at last solved the mystery. "Canned white man!" he concluded.

Emily enjoyed her stay at the camp. "There is a sense of isolation in the woods that you do not find to be loneliness. A large part of the pleasure is to discover that you can not only live without the modern conveniences and amusements of the city, but that you are really happier without them."

But the Murphys' life in the country was coming to an end. After four years, Arthur wanted to try his hand at a different business. He sold the timber limit and invested in a coal mine in Alberta. A reluctant Emily began packing for the move to Edmonton.

At 40, with her children grown up and independent, Emily would start on a new phase of her life. She would no longer have time for writing: her work with people would take precedence.

# Chapter 6
# Life Begins at 40

E dmonton, 1907, had a population of only 14,000, but it was growing rapidly. As many as 10,000 transients a month surged through the town on their way to other places. Some stayed and swelled the crowded and noisy streets where people on foot and on horseback mingled with the traffic of trolleys and carts, barouches and bicycles. Only three years before, Jasper Avenue had been a muddy horse trail. But no one looked to the past, for Westerners believed that the future belonged to them. They were building a new society out of the wilderness.

Alberta was the last virgin frontier in North America. When it was made a province in 1905, its population was 170,000. By 1914 this number had more than doubled to 400,000. During these growth years of soaring immigration, construction went ahead at an astounding rate. Railways spread over the land followed by farms and urban centres which required schools, hospitals and offices.

From all over the world – China, Japan, Russia, Europe and America – came immigrants speaking different languages, practising different customs. Life was chaotic and disorganized. The province of Alberta was so new, its towns had grown so fast, that laws and public services could not keep pace with the changes. Great extremes in wealth soon appeared. Fortunes were made and lost overnight in land and mining speculation. Those who were thrust into poverty by ruined crops or shady business deals were left to fend for themselves, for the mood of the times echoed, "Every man for himself, and let the devil take the hindmost!" Such was the climate of Edmonton when the Murphys arrived.

Upon hearing of the arrival of Emily Murphy, author of the Janey Canuck books, many people in Edmonton wanted to meet her. Fluttering through her letter box came invitations to attend afternoon teas, picnics, horse races and balls. The wealthy women of Edmonton had invented many diversions to pass the time. But these diversions were not enough to occupy Emily. She rode out alone across the prairies, stopping at farms to chat with the wives of homesteaders. Sensing the isolation of these women, she suggested they organize weekly meetings to talk together, discuss books and ideas, and plan group projects.

During one of these visits, she heard the following story: "A farmer made entry for a homestead and his wife built the houses, out-buildings, and fences on it, and bought the implements with money she had saved from school teaching. The first year, their crop was frozen; the second, it was hailed out; and the third, a spark from the threshing-machine burned their wheat stacks. Their horses died and they had to incur debt for others. All this time, the woman supported the household with the returns from her poultry yard and dairy. Her husband finally decided to sell the farm and go to town to keep a boarding-house. The woman is opposed to the move and has been in town trying to protect her interests in the property. She finds she is unable to do so."

*Edmonton in 1906 from the roof of the Castle Hotel*

That the woman should lose the farm to her husband and be left

923.C.

*Life Begins at 40*

*A homestead near Edmonton.*

with nothing was an injustice that Emily could not accept. Determined to do something about it, she went to the library to consult books on the legal rights of women. She discovered that in the province of Alberta married women had no rights except one – the right of support from her husband. She could not own property, nor keep money she earned – it belonged to the husband – and she was denied custody of her children. As far as the law was concerned, "The husband and wife are one and that one is the husband." When a man died without leaving a will, his wife could receive no part of the estate, even if she had earned the money in the first place.

These customs went back hundreds of years and had their roots in English common law which prevailed in all of Canada but Quebec. Only by passing Canadian statutes could English common law be reversed. This meant that women would have to win their rights

**Life Begins at 40**

*A young R.B. Bennett, Calgary member of the Alberta Legislature, agreed to introduce the bill that would become the Dower Act of 1911.*

through a series of laws each granting a specific personal or political right.

Property law is a provincial concern. The new province of Alberta had no laws relating to women's property rights or the protection of children. At the time of Emily's arrival in Edmonton, the first Parliament of Alberta was in session and the Rutherford government was framing a law to give women some dower rights. But Mrs. Murphy objected to the proposed bill because it did not go far enough.

Emily had stepped right into the heart of *the* controversy surrounding women's rights in Alberta. The province was a pioneer community where women worked as hard as men in building up a farm. Naturally the question of homestead laws was the most vital issue concerning the majority of women. Emily began receiving hundreds of letters from farmers' wives who supported her efforts on their behalf.

Spurred on by the reaction of these women, and realizing the enormous importance of the issue, Emily went ahead on her own to challenge the proposed bill. She prepared herself for the fight by reading legal books recommended by her brothers. She visited the legislature to watch the procedures in arguing for a new law. Armed with facts, she then took her case right to the top. She approached the Attorney General, the Honourable Charles W. Cross. He listened politely to her demands, but it was obvious he had no intention of doing anything.

Emily would not give up. She then stationed herself in the corridors of the legislature, stopping politicians on their way in and out of the building, trying to gain their support so they would introduce and vote for her bill. At last, one young man agreed to sponsor it. He was R.B. Bennett, member for Calgary.

The day arrived for the bill to be discussed in the House. Emily attended the meeting and was asked to address the assembly. The only woman present, she rose from her seat and outlined her demands. They were modest enough. A wife must be entitled to a third of her husband's estate during his lifetime and after his death even if he leaves no will. It must be impossible for him to will away her third of the estate. (It was not until 1922 that Alberta gave married women the same rights as single women – that of being able to own property in their own names.)

Emily had spoken well and with confidence, but most men in 1910 were not ready to grant women rights. The general feeling was, "If you say yes to this, who knows what the women will want next!" The bill was thrown out on second reading.

*C. W. Cross*

Help arrived from an unexpected source. Newspapers took up Emily's cause, bringing public attention to it and helping to revive the issue. A year later the bill was again discussed in the legislature. Incorporating most of the changes demanded by Emily Murphy, the Dower Act of 1911 was finally passed. It marked Emily's first political victory. Her reputation as a forceful leader in the field of women's rights was now established.

# Chapter 7
# The Organizer

Encouraged by the successful passage of the Dower Act, Emily turned her attention to other reforms. To bring about any changes, Emily had to fight the prevailing attitude that reforms were a ridiculous idea. "Sentimental flapdoodle," declared some.

Additional laws were needed to protect the rights of women and children. Prison inmates and young offenders suffered from a system that encouraged punishment and detention rather than rehabilitation. Mental institutions were inadequately staffed and their patients were subjected to barbaric treatment.

Emily's strong sense of justice made her the defender of all people whose rights had been denied. Most of her campaigns, therefore, had legal or political implications. She embarrassed local and government officials by publicly exposing corruption and inefficiencies in the operation of prisons, hospitals and mental institutions. In this period, Emily worked with the government on a bill known as the Children's Protection Act. This act, along with the Juvenile Delinquents' Act of the Criminal Code, were the two statutes governing juvenile courts.

Emily Murphy was a reformer, not a radical, yet her campaigns certainly threatened the male establishment. By speaking out on controversial questions, she managed to influence the thinking of many people. Newspapers gave publicity to her causes and supported her on most issues. Her reputation as a journalist, reformer, and advocate of women's rights was spreading beyond Alberta into the rest of Canada.

Convinced that women could be a powerful force in changing society if they organized into action groups, Emily began using her tea parties in Edmonton as a way of enlisting socially prominent women to work for the benefit of all women. She was an excellent organizer. From her experience as a parson's wife she knew how to co-ordinate groups of women to work together for a common goal. She had a natural gift for inspiring others with her energy and convictions.

Well-known to women's groups across the country, she was elected Vice President of the National Council of Women. From 1913 to 1920 she was also National President of the Canadian Women's Press Club – a group of poets, authors and journalists. In this club, Emily met other women who shared her goals. Among them were Nellie

McClung of Winnipeg, and Helen MacGill of Vancouver.

Because of her interest in the lives of rural women, who represented the majority of women in the prairies, Emily initiated a new organization called the Federated Women's Institute. This was a union of rural women which came into existence, with Emily as its president, with a national membership of 100,000. Later the organization spread to England and the United States.

In setting up the Institute, Emily persuaded wives of prominent politicians and provincial premiers to assume honorary positions. Their names gave the organization a certain amount of power and influence so that its demands were listened to with respect both in Ottawa and the provinces. But the group tended to be conservative. The wives had to think of their husbands' reputations, so it became increasingly clear that without the vote, and without being able to run for public office, women were powerless to achieve all their goals. In 1913, a new group was formed in Edmonton for the sole purpose of getting the vote for women. Emily joined this group, The Equal

*Initial meeting of the Women's Canadian Club of Edmonton, 1911. Emily was the first president.*

**The Organizer**

Franchise League, and began working closely with Nellie McClung who had been an active member of the Political Equality League in Winnipeg, Manitoba.

The standard argument against enfranchising women, aside from quoting St. Paul in the Bible, was that the family would suffer. Many men feared that women would become too independent and neglect their husbands and children. In reaction to this point of view, early feminists protested that they had no intention of sabotaging the institutions of marriage and the family. This is why they stressed the importance of motherhood and did not concentrate solely on reforms affecting women.

In terms of numbers, it was only a small group of Canadian women who actually fought for the vote and for reforms. The indifference of most women was often discouraging. But Emily and others like her persisted in their efforts. They had a strong social conscience and felt it was their duty to be active in public affairs. Small groups of women all over the world shared this view.

*Nellie McClung*

When Emmeline Pankhurst, leader of the militant suffrage movement in Britain, came in 1911 on a speaking tour of Canada, she made her headquarters in the West at the home of Emily Murphy. The two women had much in common and soon became friends. They exchanged information and discussed tactics concerning their common cause.

Newspapers in Canada had carried sensational stories about the British suffragettes and their terrorist methods. To defend themselves against the violence that frequently erupted at demonstrations, special teams of women became expert in judo. Accused of treason, several of the movement's leaders had to leave the country under assumed names and go into hiding in France. Young women were making bombs in their rooms and going out to blow up mail boxes. Others burned down buildings and smashed windows.

Hundreds of women went to jail where they protested by going on hunger strikes. They were brutally force fed by prison guards. In contrast, the Canadian struggle for women's rights was conducted in a relatively conventional manner through existing political channels.

*Emmeline Pankhurst, centre, with Nellie McClung on the left and Emily Murphy at right*

Mrs. Pankhurst made it clear that British suffragettes had only resorted to militant methods when all other methods failed. "Our object is to annoy, to harass, to inconvenience the Government till it finds it easier to give us the vote than to fight us further." She added that men were more concerned with property than they were with people, so only by destroying property would women be able to strike at men where it hurt most.

This idea was shared by a New Zealand woman, Dr. Willoughby Ayson, who said, "Women's influence tends to balance out the growing commercialism of the age. With them the almighty dollar weighs less than human lives." New Zealand had granted all women, including Maori women, the right to vote in 1893.

Alberta, along with other Prairie provinces, had always been more liberal toward women than had the rest of Canada. It was the first province to elect a woman to the legislature, the judiciary, and closely followed British Columbia in an appointment to the cabinet. The new political party, The United Farmers of Alberta, loyally supported their women in petitioning for the vote. Farming communities in the United States had also been among the first to grant female suffrage. Perhaps it was in recognition of women's heroic qualities in enduring and overcoming the hardships of pioneer life. The contribution they made in building homesteads and running farms made them equal in value with their husbands. Another reason was that many of the women who migrated to the West were unusually adventurous and had a strong interest in public affairs.

In 1914, the Equal Franchise League of Edmonton presented a petition to the Liberal government demanding the vote for women. Premier A.L. Sifton refused to act upon the petition despite the fact that 40,000 people signed it. A year later, on March 2, 1915, Emily Murphy and Nellie McClung went to tackle the premier in person. After they left his office, he remarked on their unusual determination.

His eventual decision to grant female suffrage was based, however, on political grounds. The Liberals needed women's votes in order to win the next election. On February 24, 1916, Sifton brought forth a suffrage bill in his own name. The bill gave women complete political equality with men in all provincial, municipal and school matters. Saskatchewan and Manitoba gave women the provincial vote in the same year. All Canadian women won the right to vote in federal elections in 1919. Quebec, far behind other provinces in social reform, waited until 1940 before giving its women the provincial ballot. Feminists pointed out that all over the world, immediately following women's enfranchisement, great social reforms were introduced. In Canada, the ten-year period following women's suffrage brought about much legislation in social welfare due to the lobbying of women who wanted to change the emphasis of law from property and money to the needs of people.

*A woman winnowing wheat with a homemade sieve*

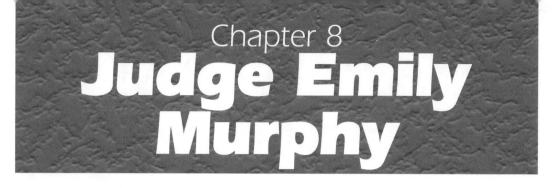

# Chapter 8
# Judge Emily Murphy

The Local Council of Women in Edmonton set up a committee to examine laws relating to the rights of women and children. Among other things, they were concerned with the treatment in court of young girls accused of vagrancy and prostitution. Two representatives of the committee were sent to the Edmonton court to watch the trials and make sure that justice was done.

Apart from the accused, they were the only females present. Just as the trial was about to begin, the Crown Prosecutor raised an objection. Stating that the cases were unfit to be heard in mixed company, he asked the two ladies to leave the court. The women replied that they represented a committee on laws concerning the protection of women and children. They had come to see that the accused were tried fairly and they had no intention of leaving. The prosecutor retaliated by saying that "ladies," such as themselves, could not possibly wish to hear sordid evidence. His words had a devastating effect. The women got up and left the courtroom in confusion. Their reaction seems strange to us now, but in those days, any public mention of sex was enough to embarrass and humiliate "decent" women. In 1916 women were rigidly separated into two groups – good and bad – based solely on their sexual behaviour. A good woman must always ignore and turn away from "evil" or she herself would become tainted by it. Once a woman committed a sexual transgression, she was forever lost and no good woman would associate with her. This old tactic of divide and conquer hindered the progress of women by splitting them against each other. In practical terms, it meant that most women had no idea of the way in which society dealt with prostitutes.

Not knowing what to do next, the two women phoned Emily Murphy for advice. Using the prosecutor's own logic against himself, Emily came up with a startling solution. If the evidence was not fit to be heard in mixed company, then the women should pressure the government to set up a special court in Edmonton where only women would be present to try other women accused of sex-related offences. It was a revolutionary idea – no woman in Canada or the entire British Empire had ever before been a judge. This fact did not deter Emily.

A few days later, she gathered up her courage and went to see the

*An immigrant woman and her children on Higgins Avenue in Winnipeg, 1907.*

attorney general of Alberta, the Hon. Charles W. Cross. He was the same man she had spoken with six years earlier in connection with the Dower Act. Naturally he remembered Murphy and knew that over the years she had become a self-taught expert on laws relating to women.

Expecting the usual evasion and resistance, Emily told him what had happened in the courtroom, then outlined her plan for a women's court. She was totally unprepared for what followed. Not only did he agree that of course there must be a women's court, he even said: "When are you ready to be sworn in as Police Magistrate?" Emily was stunned. Never had a battle been so easy.

In June, 1916, Emily Murphy was sworn in as Police Magistrate for the city of Edmonton, and Judge of the Juvenile Court. Within a year she was promoted to Magistrate for the province of Alberta.

Other appointments of women followed. Six months later, Alice Jamieson was appointed Judge in Calgary. As a member of the Local Council of Women, Mrs. Jamieson had started a suffrage campaign in Alberta back in 1910. Hearing of the appointment of two female judges in Alberta, the women of British Columbia petitioned their government to appoint a woman. In 1917, Emily's friend, Helen MacGill, was appointed Judge of the Juvenile Court in Vancouver.

Helen and Emily had much in common. Both were born into Ontario families who had been active in politics and law. Like Emily,

*Legislative Building*
*Edmonton, Alberta*

Helen's first career was in journalism. Both women used journalism as a means to publicly denounce corruption in government and law. In Vancouver, Helen had become a leading figure in many causes relating to women – equal guardianship laws, minimum wages for women, dower acts, the establishment of juvenile homes and industrial schools. Both women were respected for their extensive knowledge in the legal field.

Rapid changes had taken place in such a few short years. As recently as 1913, an editorial in *Saturday Night* magazine condemned the idea of a woman even being eligible for jury duty: "Imagine a clean-minded, good woman, a bride of a month, or the mother of a young family, sitting as a jury woman upon a dirty, filthy, criminal court case."

Although women were being granted more rights than before, the emotional attitude toward them working in a man's world had not altered much. From the start, Emily faced much opposition. On her first day in court, with confused prisoners addressing her as "Your Majesty" or "Sir," Emily had to contend with a lawyer who refused to accept her authority as judge on the grounds that she was a woman.

The case, involving a breach of the Liquor Act, was just about to begin when the Counsel for the Defence rose to his feet to object to the jurisdiction of the magistrate. Stating that a judge must be a "qualified person" he argued that only men were persons within the meaning of the statutes. Emily listened to his objection, recorded it, then continued with the trial.

Every day from then on, the same criminal lawyer raised the same objection. Other barristers caught on and repeated the charge that a woman is not a person. Emily coolly replied, "It is a poor fellow who cannot think of a new argument." She would then carry on with the proceedings.

Through her own battles for acceptance in a man's world, Emily came to sympathize with other groups of people who were denied access to positions of authority and status: African Canadians, Aboriginals, Chinese, eastern Europeans. She knew that many people did not have equal protection from the law for various reasons: often they were unaware of their rights; did not understand the formal customs or laws of Canada; spoke English poorly or not at all; or simply could not raise money for bail nor afford to hire a lawyer for their defence. Ninety percent of all criminal cases are tried in magistrate's courts, and as a result, the judges are often overworked. Emily knew that many tried to rush through the cases of those who were not able to defend themselves.

Race prejudice was strong at that time, and Emily's public defence of "foreigners" (anyone not of British descent) caused much controversy. Respectable publications such as *Saturday Night* magazine openly declared that "Canada is a white man's country and should remain so."

Emily had a wide view of her role on the bench. A judge must be fair, impartial and free from any political influence. She must make her ruling by applying legal principles to the facts in each case. But when Emily found the law to be inadequate in certain areas, she made it her job to see that the law was changed.

Strict but fair in all her judgments, she treated each offender as an individual, never allowing herself to become an extension of the impersonal legal machine. Feeling responsible for those whom she had sentenced, she visited them in prisons or in mental hospitals, and wrote letters of encouragement.

*Helen Gregory MacGill served as Judge of the Juvenile court in Vancouver for 23 years.*

**Judge Emily Murphy**

Although personally involved in the suffering of others, Emily refused to become cynical. Despite the atrocious stories she heard every day – assault, rape, child abuse, murder – she still continued to believe in each person's capacity for good. She claimed that the aim of the law was not to take revenge, but to show mercy and provide rehabilitation. She published part of the diary of a young man who had been sentenced to hang for murdering his wife. He had written, "There should come to me some severe punishment for the life I have taken, but it should be remedial in character rather than revengeful....It does not seem a good policy, nor economic, to kill a man in order to kill the evil that is in him."

*Emily conducting juvenile court, 1918*

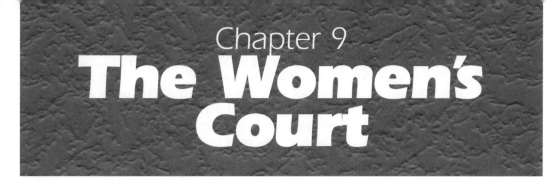

# Chapter 9
# The Women's Court

As the first woman in Canada to keep a courthouse, Emily soon learned there could be no such thing as a "woman's court" because both men and women were charged together in certain offences, such as being present in opium dens or houses of prostitution. When the main charge was against a woman, and the lesser against a man, the case would be heard in the woman's court, and vice versa.

The atmosphere of the woman's court was less official and imposing than the customary courtroom. There was no dock and the prisoner sat in an armchair before the magistrate, standing only to be sworn in and to hear the charges. Cases were tried with greater privacy – free from the curious stares of those who came in off the streets to hear personal details of the evidence. Names of the offenders were seldom made public or printed in newspapers. Emily gave each girl or woman tried a chance to change her life if she wished to make use of the opportunity. On her release from prison or training school, a trusted woman would meet the girl at the railway station to take her to a home or place of work that had previously been arranged between them.

All the staff connected with the court were women – the court orderly, two police constables, and two probation officers. The court orderly, who had previously been a matron, served summonses and accompanied the accused to court. The policewomen did preventive work such as patrolling the cabarets, dance-halls, and streets after the theatres had closed. As part of the Department of Neglected Children, the job of the probation officers was to supervise wards of the Department who were under probation. They also prepared cases for court where they could hear the cases without embarrassment and learn about the provisions of the Criminal Code, the Provincial Statutes and the City By-laws. With this knowledge they were then able to work for change when needed. Emily felt it was the responsibility of every woman to know what went on in the back streets of Edmonton. Condemning the smug attitude of those who felt superior to the suffering of "fallen women," Emily declared that everyone contained a mixture of good and bad impulses, and that the mark of a really fine woman was loyalty to her own gender. "No woman can become or remain degraded without all women suffering."

Yet she was not sentimental in her handling of these girls. "The best way a woman magistrate, or any other woman, can be a saviour, is not to stoop and save, but to stand by the girl and let her save herself." Socially prominent women came to the court and befriended the girls. Sometimes they found them jobs or took them into their homes until they could fend for themselves. The women's court became valued not just as an example of women's rights, but as a spiritual force in the community.

Day after day, a dismal procession of young girls passed before her. Frightened and desperate, often crying, they gradually responded to Emily's firm but sympathetic questioning. Homeless, with no money and no jobs, many of the girls had been forced into stealing or prostitution just to survive. Most were under 18 and had come from farms and villages to look for work in the city. When they were found wandering the streets with no money, they were charged with vagrancy – another way of picking up girls suspected of prostitution. In effect, the law made it a crime to be poor.

Some of the girls in Emily's court were innocent of any crime: they were classified as delinquent because they were pregnant and unmarried. Rejected by their families, shamed by society, they were completely alone and had nowhere to go. It was obvious to Emily that these girls should be helped and not punished.

Emily worked to establish maternity homes for unwed mothers and industrial schools that would teach a trade to young offenders. In the case of the mentally challenged, she demanded that the courts should have the services of psychiatric clinics so the magistrate could take into account the special needs of each individual before passing sentence. She insisted on a better adult probation system to keep families together rather than sending mothers or fathers to jail when their crimes were not serious.

Emily Murphy was lenient with young women, and did everything she could to avert them from a criminal career, but found that her work with older prostitutes achieved very little. Over the years, many of these women had become hardened drug addicts and no longer had the desire or will to change their lives.

Before she became a magistrate, Emily, like most Canadians, was totally unaware of the extent of drug addiction. Every day in court she saw evidence of its destruction, and she realized how it was linked with all kinds of crime. The victims of its use, "withered stalks of pain," stared at her with huge tortured eyes from ghost-like and emaciated faces. They were dazed, half awake creatures who looked "centuries old in misery." All Emily could do was sentence them to prison, knowing that some would die there and others would carry on as before as soon as they were released. As a magistrate she had to administer a law which viewed addiction as a crime. But Emily soon realized drug abuse should be treated as a disease and she criticized the Drug Law that did not provide for medical examination or treatment.

Emily decided to research the subject thoroughly and to write a series of articles that would alert the public to the dangerous and increasingly widespread use of drugs. She read books from Britain, China, India and the United States that focused on the subject. She corresponded with doctors, psychiatrists, and police chiefs all over the country. She questioned addicts in her own court to learn first-hand why they took drugs and what effect it had on them. "They see moving-pictures on the wall in which a hideous head, toothed and grizzly, appears to insult and threaten them." As well as hallucinations, Emily described the physical consequences of long-term addiction: "He ages quickly, becomes indolent, parasitical, totter-kneed, and without enough brawn to throw a puppy dog." Eventually drug addiction "degrades the morals and enfeebles the will."

Vancouver was known to be the port of entry for most of the opium from China. It used to be smuggled directly to the United States from China in tea chests, beams of vessels, under stairways, behind saloon panels and in the legs of chairs said to be family heirlooms. Since the United States had cracked down on smuggling, Canada had become the intermediary through the ports of Montreal and Vancouver. Drugs were then smuggled across the border in trains with the help of porters and customs officials.

Wanting to see for herself how the drug trade operated, Emily went with two "dope cops," plainclothes men from the RCMP, to make a raid in Vancouver's Chinatown, "that strange district where men seem to glide from nowhere to nothing."

*In entering Shanghai Alley, I was warned to stand clear of the doorways lest a rush be made from inside, where I would be trampled upon. In passing up a narrow staircase of unplanned boards, one detective walked ahead and one behind me, each carrying a flashlight....The head man stopped about midway up, and inserted a long key into a board when, to my amazement, a door opened where no door had been visible. Here, in a small cupboard, without a window – a kennel of a place – lay four opium debauchees or, as the police designate them, "hop-heads."*

*Maclean's* magazine published Emily's five articles exposing the drug situation in Canada. People were shocked by the terrifying facts she presented. Newspapers across the country followed up her comments with local stories. So intense was the interest in this formerly

*Sir Robert Borden*

unmentioned subject that, in 1922, Emily published the first comprehensive book on drug addiction in North America, *The Black Candle*.

This book shattered many popular misconceptions about drug addiction. Emily pointed out that the habit was not confined to the Chinese as certain journalists maintained. She accused them of whipping up race hatred, for the facts indicated that as many or more people of European descent were involved with drugs. It was not only the poor or the criminal element either; many rich people were also addicted. She pointed out that 15% of doctors, nurses, dentists, pharmacists and veterinarians were addicted. Police found in Edmonton a doctor who prescribed 800 emergency prescriptions in one day. Some pharmacists could only produce records for a third of the drugs shown on their invoices from the wholesaler.

In *The Black Candle*, Emily presented the medical facts in a non-emotional, non-sensational manner. She also quoted conversations with addicts about their personal experiences with drugs. Her recommendations on how to control the drug trade and how to treat addicts were adopted by some provinces. She was considered an authority on the subject and was asked to speak at public gatherings throughout Canada and the United States. The League of Nations ordered many copies of the book for its committee on narcotics traffic. Sir Robert Borden, then president of the Canadian delegation to the League of Nations, invited Emily to serve on one of the committees.

She demanded that federal and provincial governments share the cost of treating an addict in hospital rather than imposing a prison term; that there should be follow-up programs to employ an ex-addict in an area removed from the influence of old friends; that sentences for peddling drugs should be more severe; that doctors should be limited in the amount of drugs they could prescribe to each patient; that all drugs should be obtained from the government, and a record should be kept from the time the narcotic left the importer, to the time it was received by the consumer.

Another result of her public campaign was the Patent Medicine Act of 1919. The act banned cocaine, opium and its derivatives from use in patent medicines. Up to this time, such drugs were common ingredients in all kinds of over-the-counter medicines.

Throughout all this, people phoned or came to Emily's home seeking help or

*The Famous 5 monument by Edmonton artist Barbara Paterson, was unveiled on Parliament Hill, Ottawa, October 18, 2000*

offering information. The work she was doing was very dangerous. Threats on her life were made, but Emily refused to back down. She knew that these threats were made by people involved in the distribution of drugs who represented a highly organized network of crime syndicates. But she also knew that other groups, whose members had political influence, were threatening her. These people wanted the drug situation to worsen so they could blame it on prohibition. That way they hoped to force the government into re-opening liquor stores and bars. Emily remarked, "I notice that officials who start out intending to fight the drug traffic, have the quietus put upon them before they go very far."

# Chapter 10
# Are Women Persons?

On Emily's first day in court, a lawyer had challenged her right to be a judge on the grounds that a woman is not a person. When Alice Jamieson and Helen MacGill were appointed judges, they both met with the same objection.

The issue was based on the interpretation of the wording in Canada's written Constitution, the British North America Act. The Act uses the word "persons" when speaking in the plural, and "he" in the singular. In common usage, we assume that the pronoun "he" includes females. But because women had traditionally few rights and little status under the law, some men interpreted it to mean that "qualified persons" eligible for public office referred to men only. By referring to this technical loophole, they expressed their desire to exclude women from public office.

But times had changed. All women had the federal vote. Some were elected to provincial and federal legislatures – Agnes Macphail in Ottawa, Mary Ellen Smith in British Columbia, Louise McKinney in Alberta. Three women were judges and some were lawyers.

In 1920, a lawyer in the Calgary court refused to accept the authority of Judge Alice Jamieson. He appealed to Alberta's Supreme Court to rule on the question of whether a woman is a person according to law. Basing his decision on common law, which is founded on reason and good sense, the Hon. Mr. Justice Scott pointed out that the law is a living thing and should change with changing social customs. Women had shown themselves capable of performing well in public office, therefore, in his opinion, they were most definitely persons. Naturally Alberta women had known this all along, but they were glad it was officially recognized at last! But to Emily Murphy this was only the first step. She believed the issue was a national one and that every woman in Canada should have equal legal status. Her own position as a judge was now secure, but she would not be satisfied until all women had the same rights she did.

To begin the campaign, she decided to press for the appointment of a woman to the Senate. Appointment to the Senate is a federal matter, and Emily intended to force the federal government into making a national stand on the issue of women as persons.

Canada's Constitution consisted of English common law, decisions made by judges, Acts of the British and Canadian Parliament (Statutes), unwritten customs and the written part, the British North America Act of 1867. This Act outlines the distribution of legislative powers between the federal and provincial governments. Each province was a partner in the Act, so each province needed to agree to changes in it.

Section 23 of the Act lists the qualifications of a Senator – British citizenship, possession of $4,000, and minimum age of 30. Section 24 states, "The Governor General shall from time to time in the Queen's name, summon qualified persons to the Senate." Emily wanted to know, "Does the word persons include female persons?"

The first move came in 1921 when the Montreal Women's Club asked Emily if it could nominate her for appointment to the Senate. She agreed. A petition was then sent to Prime Minister Robert Borden. He responded by saying it was impossible to have women in the Senate since they were not persons.

*Arthur Meighen*

When Arthur Meighen, the new prime minister, was elected, the club forwarded him the same petition. He said he would like to see a woman in the Senate, but his advisers told him the BNA Act would first have to be amended. It would not be easy to get the consent of all provinces to do this: another 18 years would pass before Quebec even granted its women the right to vote.

In February, 1922, an Edmonton senator died and Ottawa was flooded with requests from all over Canada to appoint Murphy to the vacancy. Prime Minister Mackenzie King promised to see that changes were made to the BNA Act so women could be admitted. In 1924, he personally repeated this promise at a meeting of the Women's Canadian Club in Calgary. He failed to keep his promise.

Three years passed. Every time a vacancy occurred in the Senate, there was a revival of interest in the appointment of Emily Murphy.

She had the support of women's groups and newspapers throughout Canada. She was a well-known national figure, respected for her Janey Canuck books, her reforms, her work as a judge, and her talent at public speaking. With thousands of people clamouring for her appointment, it did not seem democratic that the public's wishes were ignored.

By 1927, Emily decided the time had come to settle the issue once and for all. She chose four women to work with her as "interested citizens" in appealing the question. These were Nellie McClung, Irene Parlby, Louise McKinney and Henrietta Muir Edwards. Nellie McClung was a writer and politician. Irene Parlby was an elected member of the Alberta government led by the United Farmers of Alberta. This party, with its militant agrarian politics, had loyally supported the advancement of women. Although Nellie McClung belonged to the opposition, and Irene Parlby to the party in power, both agreed on issues that related to the rights and needs of women and children. Louise McKinney was a cabinet member of the UFA. She had been a temperance campaigner and organizer for the Women's Christian Temperance Union. Henrietta Muir Edwards, an active feminist, was the convenor of laws for the National Council of Women. In 1875 she had organized the Working Girls' Association in Montreal which later became the YWCA.

The five women requested a prominent lawyer, the Hon. Newton Wesley Rowell, to take their case to the Supreme Court of Canada and argue on their behalf. As former leader of the Liberal opposition in the Ontario legislature, Mr. Rowell had supported

*William Lyon Mackenzie King*

**Are Women Persons?**

bills for the enfranchisement of women in both 1916 and 1917. He agreed to represent the province of Alberta in this case and, although each province could send a lawyer to debate the question, only Quebec bothered to do so. It turned out to be a confrontation between the forward-looking province of Alberta and the tradition-bound province of Quebec.

*Prime Minister King honouring Emily Murphy, Henrietta Muir Edwards, Louise McKinney, Irene Parlby, and Nellie McClung*

    Mr. Rowell referred to the Interpretation Act of 1850 (also known as Lord Brougham's Act) that was in force at the time of Confederation. This act states that all words referring to the masculine gender should also be taken to refer to the feminine gender, unless specifically stated otherwise. The Dominion Elections Act of 1920 quoted this Act when it declared that the word "persons" in Section 41 of the

**Are Women Persons?**

*Newton Wesley Rowell*

British North America Act must be interpreted to include females. As a result of the 1920 Act, women became eligible for election to the House of Commons. Mr. Rowell summed up by saying that times had changed and the law should adapt to changing social conditions. The Quebec counsel disagreed, arguing that at the time of Confederation, no one intended women to hold public office.

The debate continued for five weeks. On April 24, 1928, the five judges of the Supreme Court announced their carefully considered opinion. Basing their verdict on conditions existing at the time of Confederation, they declared that women were not persons.

Canadian women were stunned. Emily and her co-appellants were bitterly disappointed. But they were politically wise. Not wanting to spoil their chances in the final appeal, they did not denounce the Supreme Court or protest against its decision. Publicly they said, "We are sure the Supreme Court gave its judgment in all sincerity."

The five women had prepared themselves for the possibility of a negative decision. Undeterred, they planned to take their case to the highest court of appeal, the Judicial Committee of the Privy Council in England. (Only after 1949 did Canada's Supreme Court become the highest Court of Appeal for Canadians.)

Mr. Rowell went to England to present the case of these five determined Alberta women. Days passed, then weeks, then months. Members of the Privy Council were giving the matter a great deal of thought. Finally, on October 18, 1929, newspapers carried the headlines: CANADAN WOMEN WIN RIGHT TO SENATE SEATS; LONG FIGHT ENDS; JUDICIAL COMMITTEE REVERSES FINDING OF CANADA'S SUPREME COURT.

The judgment was of great interest, not only because of its constitutional implications, but because of its effect upon the status of women. Recognizing its importance, Lord Sankey, the Lord Chancellor of Great Britain, departed from normal procedure by reading the judgment in full before the court. Agreeing with Mr. Rowell, he quoted the Interpretation Act of 1850 that declared the word "persons" to mean both male and female. He added that it was a mistake on the part of Canada's Supreme Court to base its verdict on Roman law and early English decisions, concluding, "The exclusion of women from all public offices is a relic of days more barbarous than ours." (Ironically, it was not until 1957 that British women were permitted to sit in the House of Lords.)

The reaction of Canadian ministers to Britain's decision was not exactly enthusiastic. Mr. King declined to comment except to say he was pleased. Sir Robert Borden said it was essentially a judicial matter and he had nothing more to add.

Agnes Macphail, the only woman in the House of Commons, was more emphatic. "I am glad that women have been recognized as per-

*Lord Chancellor Sankey on his way to deliver the judgment that women are "persons," 1929*

**Are Women Persons?**

*Agnes C. Macphail, first woman member of the House of Commons*

sons equally with men. It is nonsense that it was not done long ago." Then she added "The women of the West have done a great deal in this and the women of the whole nine provinces should be grateful."

Emily Murphy was elated by the successful outcome. Thirteen years had passed since that first day in court when a lawyer had challenged her appointment to the bench merely because she was a woman. Through hard work and persistence, she had finally ensured that no woman in Canada would ever again suffer from that particular form of discrimination.

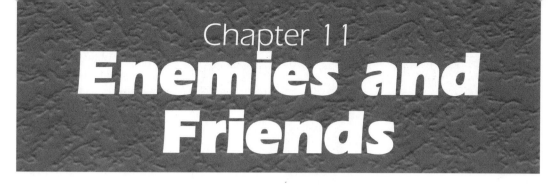

# Chapter 11
# Enemies and Friends

The Senate was, and still is, a subject of controversy. It is made up of people who are not popularly elected, but appointed by the prime minister in power. Often the prime minister chooses his own political supporters for the job, people who have contributed money to the party, or who have worked in politics for years and are ready to retire. As a result, the average age of Senators often exceeds 70.

*R.B. Bennett*

The Senate was originally created to protect provincial interests by including members appointed from each province. Its function is to discuss and approve bills originating in the House of Commons. But the real power in government lies with the elected members in the Commons and not in the Senate.

Agnes Macphail had often said in the 1920s that the Senate was a ridiculous institution and a menace to good government. Emily felt that women could abolish the Senate if they wanted because they had the vote. But as long as it existed, she believed that women should receive equal consideration for Senatorial positions.

Since 1921, when the issue of having women in the Senate was first raised, thousands of people across the country had named Emily Murphy as their choice. She was widely known and respected for her knowledge of law, her work in community welfare, and her

*Senator Cairine R. Wilson*

writing on public issues. She was supported by the National Council of Women, the Federated Women's Institute, and the Quebec branch of the Women's Christian Temperance Union. She also had the editorial approval of newspapers throughout Canada.

Right from the start, Nellie McClung had worked hard for Emily's appointment. "The only objection that any person can have to Mrs. Murphy for the Senate is that she is a woman....She can qualify in a dozen different ways, each one of them far beyond the qualifications of the average Senator." Since Emily had campaigned so selflessly to get women officially declared "persons," it seemed a logical reward that she should have the honour of being Canada's first woman Senator.

It did not happen that way. In 1930, one year after the Privy Council's ruling made women eligible for the Senate, the King government announced it was finally appointing a woman. Her name was Cairine Wilson. On hearing the news, many people were shocked that Murphy had been passed over in favour of a woman who had not even been involved in the long struggle waged by the five women of Alberta.

Emily was naturally disappointed, but she was glad at least that a woman had been chosen. Cairine Wilson had been prominent in women's organizations in the East and she had worked for years for the Liberal party. Her appointment by the King government was a reward for party service. Emily was a Conservative.

A month later, the King government was defeated and R.B. Bennett came to power. He was the young lawyer who had first sponsored Emily's Dower Act 20 years before in the Alberta House. An Edmonton Senator died in 1931 and various groups petitioned the government to appoint Emily Murphy.

Mr. Bennett refused. He argued that the late Senator was a Roman Catholic and he felt the successor should be of the same faith. Emily protested that the BNA Act made no reference to religion. But Mr. Bennett had made up his mind.

Emily must have been bitterly disillusioned. She had a strong sense of justice and the actions of two prime ministers who had used weak excuses for not appointing her revealed a vindictive attitude. They were probably afraid she would cause too much change and trouble within the Senate.

Discussing the value of the Senate, Grattan O'Leary wrote the following in *Maclean's*, January 1928:

*In the crimson-cushioned halls of that cathedral-like chamber, the air is warm and heavy. It drags upon you until you wilt and your head swims, and the faces of its members grow hazy. In that indolent atmosphere, so remote from the vital world outside, there is an invitation to relax and grow bored and cease to care. Aged men sit heavily in their seats, mumble wearily through their business, compressed and dull and discouraged.*

No doubt the prime ministers were right: Emily Murphy would have caused too much trouble!

# Chapter 12
# Last Days

*Arthur Murphy*

It was autumn, October 26, 1933. The morning sun stared through Emily's window, its light awakening her. She rose from bed, walked to the window and leaned out to look down at the garden bathed in a clear morning light. Sniffing the fresh faint smell of wet leaves and earth, feeling the sun warming her skin, Emily knew it was a day for being outdoors.

An hour later, she was moving along the familiar streets of Edmonton, smiling and saying hello to the people who had become her friends over the years. Sometimes she stopped to talk on the sidewalk for a few moments before moving on. Her steps had led her by habit toward the police station and court house. It was two years since she had retired as a judge, but this morning she decided to go inside and visit old colleagues.

Later, she made her way toward the library to work on several new articles. There was much research to do. Several hours passed while she sat in the reading room scanning books and newspapers and scribbling notes onto her pad. At length, satisfied she had done enough for that morning, she gathered up her coat and bag, left the library, and walked over to visit Kathleen and granddaughter Doris.

The afternoon passed while the women sat out in the back garden drinking tea and playing with young Doris. They did not go inside till the sun slipped down behind the trees, taking its warmth with it.

Evelyn drove Emily home and they had supper together with Arthur. While he was talking and joking, Emily watched his face and thought how young and strong he still looked. It was hard to believe that this man with the piercing blue eyes, the thick mane of white hair, could be 76 years old. After dinner, Arthur kissed Emily goodbye before leaving to watch a ball game in the park. Emily sat on alone for a few moments, thinking about all their years together. Then she rose from her chair and climbed the stairs to her study.

Once inside her room, she was drawn again into her private world of thought and writing. She was at home in the comfortable disorder of this room that had become her sanctuary. Piles of books were heaped on the floor, and her desk was scattered with sheaves of papers and notes, clippings and letters; but Emily knew exactly where everything was.

She sat down at the desk, sharpened a pencil, and began writing. The glow of the lamp burnished her face and made a yellow pool of light on the paper. She wrote steadily for several hours, at times pausing to think and to look out at the night sky lit by glittering stars. Around midnight, she turned out the lamp and went to bed. In the darkness she let the events of the day slip through her mind until she drifted into sleep.

During the night, Evelyn heard a short cry coming from her mother's room. She hurried out of bed and crossed the hall. She called out to her mother, but there was no response.

The next day, October 27, Emily's body was carried down to the parlour. News of her death first reached the people who lived close by, those whom Emily had known and worked with for years in Edmonton. One after another they started to arrive at the house. There was a policeman from the nearby corner, a group of nuns, a man from the Salvation Army, and a woman on welfare with a baby in her arms. Two former prostitutes whom Emily had helped brought a single rose, which they placed in the coffin. It was a fitting token to go to the grave with Judge Emily Murphy. Her daughters left it there, knowing that Emily would have appreciated that gesture, perhaps more than any other.

# Emily Murphy

|  |  |
|------|-------|
| 1868 | Born in Cookstown, Ontario |
| 1887 | Marries Arthur Murphy |
| 1898 | Goes to England |
| 1899 | Returns to Canada and settles in Toronto |
| 1901 | *Impressions of Janey Canuck* is published |
| 1903 | Moves to Swan River, Manitoba |
| 1907 | Moves to Edmonton, Alberta |
| 1910 | *Janey Canuck in the West* is published |
| 1911 | Dower Act of 1911 is passed giving Alberta women property rights |
| 1912 | *Open Trails* is published |
| 1914 | *Seeds of Pine* is published<br>Becomes Vice President of the National Council of Women |
| 1916 | Alberta women get the vote<br>Becomes first woman Police Magistrate and Judge of the Juvenile Court |
| 1922 | *The Black Candle* is published |
| 1929 | October 18 England's Privy Council declares Canadian women "persons" |
| 1930 | Cairine Wilson is first woman appointed to Senate |
| 1931 | Retires from bench |
| 1933 | Dies on October 27 in Edmonton |